KÜ

HEALING IN OUR TIME

ELISABETH KÜBLER-ROSS, M.D.

EDITED BY GÖRAN GRIP, M.D.

STATION HILL OPENINGS

BARRYTOWN, LTD.

Published under the Station Hill Openings imprint by Barrytown, Ltd., Barrytown, N.Y. 12507.

Distributed by Consortium Book Sales & Distribution, Inc. 1045 Westgate Drive, Saint Paul, MN 55114-1065.

Text and cover design by Susan Quasha.

The talk in this book has been excerpted from *Death is Of Vital Importance*, Copyright by Elisabeth Kübler-Ross, Station Hill Press, 1995.

A Swedish version of *Death is Of Vital Importance* has been published by Bokförlaget Natur och Kultur under the title *Döden är livsviktig: Om livet, döden och livet efter döden*, Copyright 1991 by Elisabeth Kübler-Ross.

Library of Congress Cataloging-in-Publication Data

Kübler-Ross, Elisabeth.
    Healing in our time / Elisabeth Kübler-Ross ; edited by Göran Grip.
        p.   cm. – (Kübler-Ross in person)
    Excerpted from: Death is of vital importance, 1995.
    ISBN 1-886449-26-0 (lg. Print)
    1. Death.   2. Life.   3. Future life.   4. Spiritual life.
I. Grip, Göran. II. Title. III. Series: Kübler-Ross, Elisabeth.
Kübler-Ross in person.
    [BD444.K793   1997]
    155.9'37—DC21   96-48974
                                                          CIP

Printed in the United States of America

Contents

The Paralyzed Woman 5

The Black Cleaning Woman 13

The Schnook 20

Bernie Siegel 36

Chemotherapy 39

The Gnomes 43

The Workshops 45

Christ 48

Dougy Again 51

ABOUT THIS BOOK

Elisabeth Kübler-Ross' words, spoken at the spur of the moment, have been edited here with the aim of creating a readable text. We have taken pains, however, to preserve the quality of immediate presence that is characterized by the author's special magnetism, the power of direct address to a live audience for which she is renowned. We think there is a special meaning in presenting Elisabeth Kübler-Ross "live" on the subject of death and dying — and that this is a key to her message.

This book has been adapted from Elisabeth Kübler-Ross' tape-recorded lecture, *Healing in Our Time,* delivered in Washington, in 1982.

Healing in Our Time

(Elisabeth is not the first one to give her speech at this seminar. A man introduces her somewhat solemnly, "We thank the beautiful people who have organized this seminar for bringing into our midst . . . one of the loveliest, most distinguished women of our age. This woman has received much love. This woman has given much love. Elisabeth Kübler-Ross, you are a celebrator of life, and you honor us with your presence. Thank you!") (Applause)

(Elisabeth starts a little hesitantly): Thank you... Thank you... Thank you... It's very touching . . . to see so many people . . . and to see how people are ready. . . for a lot of new things to come. I don't know how many of you followed what was said since eight o'clock . . . I didn't! *(surprised laughter from audience)*

But that is how it should be! I'm not saying that with any negative connotation. We are in such an exciting time where so many new things are coming up that I don't think any single individual person understands what Olga is doing, what Selma is doing, what Elmer is doing — what I am doing.

Many people who don't understand what we are doing say that we are crazy, and that we are psychotic, or that we have lost our reality testing, or also they give us some very funny labels. And if you get those labels, regard it as a blessing *(surprised silence and then warm laughter and applause)* regard it as a blessing. I am naturally psychotic *(laughter)* all the time — if you define reality testing in a very limited manner, in only understanding the things that happen to all people and are understood by all people.

There is a beautiful poster in my office that says, "To avoid criticism: say nothing, do nothing, be nothing." That is one choice that people have. You people who are in this audience do not belong to that group. But that does not make you superior — I hope you hear that also. Because a child who goes to high school would not knock a brother or a sister who is in kindergarten.

We are beginning to see that life in its physical form is literally nothing but a school where we learn, where we grow, where we have to pass a lot of tests. And the higher up we get in the evolution, the tougher the tests. Then we will also begin to understand that nobody is a teacher, that nobody is a student; we have just students at different levels.

Why do I say all this? When I listen to statements [from a previous lecture] like, "the normal brain limits our awareness" all I can write down is, "Thank God!" *(surprised silence from audience)* And I think it gives me even more of a sense of awe about God, how well He knew man, that He created a brain that limits us. Because if the brain didn't have any limitations, then we could never take it, we could not tolerate it. It is as if man suddenly were able to have an orgasm for twenty-four hours: who would wash the dishes! *(big laughter and applause)* I don't even mean that jokingly! *(more laughter)*

It is to me a gift to be a human being, and the little children that are born now — I was visited by a three-week-old baby in my room before coming down — I look at those babies and I say, "What a miracle!" I mean, here in Washington are all these brains together: how many of you could recreate something like this baby even if you had a hundred-billion dollars? Nobody could re-create it. Nobody.

I'm spending my life with no theories about higher consciousness, but with the healing of human beings very much on the ground. And yet if I had not been on the other side, I would not be able to do what I'm doing. I would never be able to be with dying children, with parents of murdered children, with the mother who stepped out to get the bottle of milk and came back to find her three sons shot in the neck, with a couple who lost all their children from cancer within six months, with a young physician who watched his father die of Huntington's disease at age forty becoming senile, watched him for years and years and years wondering, "Am I one of the fifty percent in the family who will get it also?" then beginning to develop symptoms and looking at his preschool children, knowing that in three years he too would be like his father was a few years before his death. And the only solution this man can think of is suicide.

I could never work eighteen hours a day, seven days a week, seeing anguish, agony and pain and horror if I could not see the other side of the coin also. And if people began to learn the meaning of life, and the meaning even of the pain, and the meaning even of the tragedies, and the incredible miracle of human life, then they would bless it every day, not only the joys and the heights but, especially, perhaps the difficult periods of time.

The Paralyzed Woman

I received a phone call some time ago from a young nurse, who, out of loving care, had promised her mother to take her home to die if she should ever become anything close to a vegetable, or if she should become dependent on machines, because in their definition this would not be living. They promised each other to totally and fully live and love as long as they were in their physical bodies. I asked her why she called and she said, "All I wanted to ask is one little favor, and that is that you talk to my mother, because today is the last day that she can speak."

Her mother had a rapidly progressing neurological disease and they could see how the paralysis progressed from day to day from her toes on up, and they knew almost to the day when she would no longer be able to speak, then no longer be able to breathe. By then, she would have to choose to exist on a respirator or actually die. This was the last day that she would be able to speak.

I thought that that was a very simple request so I said, "Sure, put the telephone on your mother's ear." She put it on her ear, and the mother tried to speak, and I absolutely did not understand what she tried to say. If you live with people it is easier, but over the telephone it was totally impossible. It is very important that we are honest, that we do not pretend that we understand children or patients when we don't.

So I told the daughter, "I don't know what she is talking about, but she has some very important unfinished business that she needs to share. Unfortunately I'm leaving for Europe." And I asked her impulsively, "How far away do you live?" She said, "Four hours from where you are." I said, "That's too bad. If it were three hours, I could make it back and forth in six. Eight hours is impossible. I have to catch a plane." And then, impulsive as I am, I said, "But I do believe in miracles. If I need to see your mother I'll be able to see her. One possibility is that you put her in a van" (she was paralyzed up to her neck) "and you hit the road towards where I live and I come from the other way and we will make a 'street corner consultation'." (laughter) I don't know a better name for it, but I do that all the time. As long as you know your geography, it works.

And this young daughter, who happened to be a nurse said, "I believe in miracles too. My mother's house is on the other side of Los Angeles and if I bring her there, you can make it in time and still catch your plane for Switzerland."

All I needed to do was to find a friend who was not afraid of cops *(laughter)* and who could really, you know, speed to Los Angeles. We hopped into a car, we were almost flying to L.A.

I walked into this woman's house. And you know how we project our own expectations. I expected a fifty-five year old woman, which was my age at that time, to be in bed, paralyzed up to the neck, depressed, miserable and unhappy. And when I walked in I saw that she had the biggest beaming smile all over her face.

I tried to talk to her and to figure out what she was trying to tell me. This is what she was saying: She wanted to thank me for making it possible for her to die at home. She had been taken home by her daughter and if she had not been at one of my lectures, she would have been on a respirator now, and that would not have been such a horrible nightmare, though very unpleasant. But then she would have been cheated out of the greatest gift of her life which was the presence of her new grandchild, who was born twelve weeks earlier. She said, "We would never have been able to see each other. Because we still have those signs in the hospital: 'No children allowed'."

She wanted to thank me. I said, "Tell me what it was like, so I can pass it on, what it was like that night when you knew that the next morning you would no longer be able to move your arms and your fingers. What was it like? A few months ago you could walk around in the garden, take care of everything. "And now she was literally dead up to her neck.

And again instead of making a long, sad, tragic face, drowning herself in very understandable self-pity, she had an even bigger smile and she said (all her communications were with the help of a speaking board!), "I have to tell you what happened. Because the morning I woke up and my arms were paralyzed, then everything was paralyzed up to my chin. My daughter realized the situation and walked into my room and very quietly put this three-month-old baby in my paralyzed arms. And I simply watched her. Suddenly this little girl lifted up her fingers and her hands and her arms and discovered them. I said to myself: 'What an incredible blessing. I had it for fifty-five years, and now I can pass it on to my granddaughter.'"

Then she started to drool, and since I am an old meany I said, "Drooling like this! Brrr!" I said, "I'm sure a few months ago you would not have liked having visitors watching you drool like this all over the place." And she laughed and said, "You are damned right. A few months ago I wouldn't want anybody to see me this way. But you know what? Now the two of us drool together and laugh together." (laughter from audience)

In a very brief nutshell, this is what I'm trying to share with you: you do not appreciate the gifts you have. Very few of you appreciate that you can go to the bathroom, that you can walk, that you can dance, that you can sing, that you can laugh. You have to wait until you lose it, and then you bless what you had in a past tense.

If you reached higher consciousness, can you imagine how tragic it would be? Because you would not appreciate what you have unless it happens for a few glimpses of a moment just to give you a taste of what you could have all the time once you appreciate what you already have. Does that make sense?

It is very simple. Anybody and everybody can heal. Anybody and everybody can have every degree of higher consciousness. And you do not need to do anything about it, except appreciate what you have and get rid of the things that block you from fully appreciating what you have. And I will tell you in very plain, practical language how to do that.

Do not look for gurus or babas. The teachers you will get in your life are the most unlikely people in the world. In the years that I started my work on death and dying at the University of Chicago I was very much a *persona non grata*. People would spit at me and humiliate me in public because I was a physician who tried to work with dying patients. It was very difficult and very painful and very lonely and very hard *(with the slightest pain in her voice)*. They called me the v.. vul.. vulture. It seems like a hundred years ago.

When you are very alone, very isolated, and you walk on very thin ice, you have to be very careful, you will have to know exactly how far you can go before the ice breaks. It is literally a question of be or not to be. If you go too fast too soon you lose everything you have gained. This is also true when you try to share with other people about experiences of higher consciousness. If you are not sure, go slow. And if you are still not sure, then keep quiet. Because it just means that those who are listening to you are not yet ready for it. And that is OK!

It was very difficult. I had nobody to support me. I was in a very difficult, precarious life situation and it was only the patients who supported me. They gave me the message: you are at the right place, continue to do it. Every patient would kind of sustain me to the next one, and then to the next one. During that very vulnerable time I became a very good psychiatrist because I was hyperalert as to whom to trust and whom to go very slowly with.

In those days, when I was very alone, I really needed moral support. The hospital chaplains had not yet associated and I was there alone except for one woman, a black cleaning woman.

The Black Cleaning Woman*

The black cleaning is greatest teacher. I have to give her credit for what I have learned as long as I live. *She* is the one to

---

*Since my stroke, I can no longer recall the name of this woman or of many other people who have been important to me.

...et credit for it. And she doesn't know how much she did.

This black cleaning woman in the university hospital had a gift that was totally beyond my comprehension. She was totally uneducated and had never been to high school and certainly had no academic understanding. But there was something about her, and I didn't know what it was. I was dying to know what in the world she did with my dying patients. Every time she walked into the room of one of my dying patients something happened in that room. And I would have given a million dollars to learn that woman's secret.

One day I saw her in the hallway. I said to myself, "You always tell your medical students: if you have a question, for Heaven's sake ask," and I gave myself a big push and quickly approached her. I said to her, rather curtly, "What are you doing with my dying patients?" (laughter from audience)

Of course she became paranoid and very defensive, and she said, "I'm not doing anything, I'm only cleaning the room." *(amusement from audience)* I came from Switzerland, so I couldn't understand that a black cleaning woman would have a problem talking to a white professor of psychiatry.

I said to her, "That's not what I'm talking about." But she didn't trust me and walked away.

We snooped around each other for weeks *(laughter)*. You know what snooping around means? This is the simplest example of symbolic nonverbal language. That is what people do who try to get to know each other, who try to find out who you really are, not what you wear or your external form.

After weeks of snooping around like this, she had the courage to just grab me and drag me into a back room behind the nursing station. There she opened her heart and her soul to me and told me a very dramatic story, which to me was totally disconnected with my question and was totally beyond *my* intellectual comprehension. I had no idea at that time what was going on.

She told me how she grew up on 63rd Street in a very bad, bad, poor neighborhood. No food, very sick children, no medicines. On one occasion she sat in the county hospital with her three-year-old boy on her lap, desperately waiting hours for a physician to come, and watching her little boy die of pneumonia in her arms.

And the issue about this woman was that she shared all this pain and agony without hate, without resentment, without anger, and without negativity. In those days I was very naive, and I was just ready to say to her, "Why are you telling me all this? What has this to do with my dying patients?" And as if she could read my mind she said, "You see, Dr. Ross, death is not a stranger to me anymore. He is like an old, old acquaintance. I am not afraid of him anymore. Sometimes when I walk into the room of your dying patients, they look so scared. I can't help but walk over to them and touch them and say, 'It's not so terrible.'"

If it had not been for this woman — and I mean that from the bottom of my heart in the most concrete way — if it had not been for that woman, I do not think I would have lasted. This is what I'm trying to say: do not look for gurus or babas. Your teachers come disguised. They come in the form of children, they come in the form of senile, old grandmas, and they come in the form of a black cleaning woman.

This woman does not know who she is. And she does not know what role she played and how many lives she has touched as a consequence of her choices. It does not matter *what* you do in life. The only thing that matters is that you do what you do with love.

I promoted this woman to my first assistant much to the dismay of my academic colleagues *(laughter and applause)*. Because what this woman... *(Elisabeth interrupts herself, turns to audience and very gently says)*: If you are honest: how many of you applauded out of hostility? *(surprised silence from audience)*

How many of you applauded with hostility? *(continued silence from audience)*

Hostility *against* the physicians and the establishment? *(scattered applause and laughter and finally a "Bravo!")* Yes! As long as you do that, you are responsible for things not being better *(reluctant, scattered applause)*. *(still very gently)* It is very important that you learn that. We curse, we question, we judge and we criticize, and any time we judge or criticize, we add negativity to the world.

Ask yourself why a high school kid should knock a first grader. Do you understand what I said before? It is only arrogance that makes people do that. Do I make myself clear? *(reluctant applause)*

(Very gently): If you want to *heal* the world it is terribly important to understand that *you cannot heal the world without first healing thyself.* As long as you knock and judge and criticize anybody, *you* are responsible for a Hiroshima, Nagasaki, Viet Nam, Maidaneck or an Auschwitz. And I mean that literally *(si-*

lence from audience).

In my Death and Dying seminars, to digress for a minute, we included randomly selected dying patients. I was a novice, and I depended on my patients to be the teachers and God forbid I was ever to be stuck ten minutes without a patient. I wouldn't have known what to say. That was ten thousand years ago *(laughter).* Actually only thirteen years ago.

One day my patient died ten minutes before the seminar and I had a two-hour class with nothing to talk about. And I was a novice, I mean a total novice. All the way to my classroom I was talking to everybody saying, "Please help me. What do I do for two hours? Do I just cancel the class?" But I couldn't do that because the audience came from far away and everywhere.

Then I was up on the stage and the dreaded moment had finally come when I stood in front of eighty students with no patient. That moment was one of the windstorms of my life, and it turned out to be one of the greatest lessons of my teaching about death and dying.

I asked this mixed group of medical students, theology students, OT, RT, nurses, clergy and rabbis, "You know, we don't have a patient today. Why don't we view the biggest problem we have here in this medical school and then use that problem instead of talking to a patient." I was wondering what the group would come up with. I was just gambling to kill those two hours. Much to my surprise they picked the head of one of the departments — where all the patients died. I am not saying what this department was because then the man would be recognizable.

The Schnook

The problem this physician had was that he was trained like all the rest of us: to cure, to treat, to prolong life, but he had never gotten any help beyond that. And all his patients died.

His patients were so full of metastases you could feel the tumors getting bigger and bigger. And he had developed such a defensiveness that he went too far, and told them that they were free of cancer, and that their feelings of being ill were all in their mind.

He did this to such an extent that many of his patients asked to see a psychiatrist, because if it was all in their mind, then they needed psychiatric help.

I was in charge of the psychosomatic service. I was supposed to help those patients get rid of their fear that they were full of cancer. But I could look at the X-rays and see that they were right. They did have cancer. I think you realize the horrible conflict which he put *me* in. *I* couldn't say, "It is not you but your doctor who needs a shrink." Of course I couldn't do that. *You can never help somebody by knocking somebody else. (silence from audience)*

And in an institution you have to have a certain degree of solidarity, so I couldn't tell this doctor that it was his problem...

So he was the doctor that they picked as a problem. And then I didn't know what to do with it. I absolutely... I was up on that stage with eighty people staring at me, and I thought, "What am I going to do now?"

I told them that I ... with this man... that you cannot help somebody if you feel locked with negativity towards him. There has to be some compassion or understanding or love, or at least understanding or liking of a person in order to help him. But if you are so negative that you would strangle this guy, and I would have loved to strangle him a thousand times, you cannot help him. So I told them that this could not be a patient that I could accept as a psychiatrist.

And then I asked a question to this group who consisted of clergy, rabbis, doctors, nurses, all helping professionals, "Who in this group likes him? Can those who like him put their hands up?" *Nobody* put their hands up!

And I got so desperate, and I looked at everybody and said, "Doesn't anybody like him just a little bit?" At that time a young woman put her hand up. And without realizing it I must have attacked that poor young nurse, I guess... *(laughter from audience)* ... because I looked at her and said, "Are you sick?" *(big laugh-*

I recognized her and she shared her story.

That same night this guy came again, and for two nights she tried but she just didn't have the guts. But the third night, when he came out of his last room belonging to a dying young cancer patient, she suddenly remembered what she had made a commitment to do, and her intellectual quadrant started to interfere and she said to herself, "Well, one ought not to do that." Then she said, "No, I promised not to think."

So before she started thinking she moved on her intuitive, spiritual quadrant. She said, "I just walked over to him and reached out, I didn't even physically... I think that I didn't even touch him. And I said: 'God, it must be difficult!' to him."

He grabbed her and started to sob and cry and took her into his office, and with his head in his arms, just poured out his pain, his grief, his anguish and shared with her probably more than he had shared with any other human being. He shared how for many years his friends had earned a living while he was still going to school, how he specialized, how he sacrificed, how he couldn't date, how he went into a specialty where he really, really thought that he could help somebody. At the end of the sharing he said, "And now I am the chairman of a department, and every single one of my patients dies on me." Like his total impotence. Was it worthwhile to give up his personal happiness, his relationships for this?

And all she had to do was to listen.

Do you understand that? How could you ever knock such a man?

Because of the courage of this nurse to be herself, not to think what one ought to do if one is down here and the other one is up here, but because we are all brothers and sisters, she was able for two minutes to treat him like a human being, not like Doctor Bigshot but like a human being who has the same qualities that all of us have.

One year later this man asked for consultations, but only to be given by telephone so nobody would know about it.

Before this he had never asked for a consultation from the psychiatric service because he was too arrogant to acknowledge that he needed help. Three or four years later, he asked for ordinary consultations like everybody else. And eventually he became a very humble, understanding man with so much compassion for his patients.

I think it would have killed him, he would have been burned out if he hadn't asked for help.

So, it is possible to do this with a schnook like him by just finding the right nurse. And, of course, you don't have to be a nurse. And nobody is too young to help. I hope you hear that.

How many of you hated, until this workshop, some of your doctors? *(silence from audience)* Be very honest. Every time you label somebody as a schnook, or whatever word you have, you increase that person's negativity. And the nurses are mainly responsible for the doctors being so obnoxious. I'm only talking about the obnoxious doctors now, but there are naturally also some good ones. Do you understand why I say that?

Because if a doctor is insecure in the first place and therefore thinks that he has to be very angry and act as a bigshot, and if he works in a unit where there are ten nurses who really hate his guts, then he will pick up their negativity, and that, in turn, will add to his insecurity. And that makes him become ten times more arrogant. Do you understand how powerful your thoughts are?

So if you think, "I'm gonna call this man a schnook again because he didn't do things my way," then immediately block those thoughts and surround him with love and understanding and compassion instead.

If a whole unit of staff will do that with one doctor for one week, you can actually see the change of that person's behavior without your ever saying one single word to him aloud. Have any of you ever tried that? You have no idea how powerful your thoughts are.

So if you surround such people — and the worst people naturally need it the most — with love and positive thoughts you can change the most impossible...

Do you hear what I am trying to say to you? This is the only way that you can bring about a change. And I will briefly talk as a psychiatrist because it is very important that you heal the world soon, before it is too late: *you have to understand that you cannot heal the world without healing yourself first.*

<hr>

This is what we are talking about: unfinished business. God created man perfect, to give him all the awareness he can tolerate, all the things he can use. If you cannot tolerate it, you would not be given it. You always get what you need, but not always what you want. And as you grow and evolve, you get more. Not when you want it, but when you are ready for it.

Every human being consists of four quadrants: a physical, an emotional, an intellectual and a spiritual, intuitive quadrant.

Intellectually most of us are hyper-trophic — especially in this room *(a few surprised giggles from audience)*. Spiritually we are OK. The only quadrant you never have to work with is your spiritual quad-rant. It is within you and the most im-portant reason it is not emerging is that it is blocked. Physically all of you belong to health clubs and try to do yoga exer-cises and eat vitamins and do all the right things, so I am not too worried about that. Our society's biggest problem is the emo-tional quadrant. The second develop-mental stage is the emotional quadrant which develops almost exclusively be-tween the ages of one and six. That is when you get all your basic attitudes which ruin you for life. With the empha-sis on "ruin."

If you live in harmony between the physical, emotional, intellectual and spiritual quadrants, you will not get sick. You can only get sick for three kinds of reasons: traumatic reasons, genetic reasons, and disharmony among the four quadrants. And I will talk about that, and it is relevant in healing, because by knowing that, you cannot only heal people but also prevent ill health. And I hope that in the next generation we will spend ninety percent of our energy in preventing ill-health rather than putting Band-Aids on something that could have been prevented in the first place.

When you have children that cannot speak anymore or children who are too young, we use drawings to understand their symbolic language. I will share with you what medicine is going to be like in the next five years in terms of healing, done with a box of Crayola — as an adjunct, not the only thing.

When a child is unable to speak and I need to know what he needs to know to finish his unfinished business, I will give him a sheet of paper and a box of Crayola and ask him to draw a picture. And you do not tell the child what to draw.

In five or ten minutes you know that he knows that he is dying. You know where the pathology is. If he, for example, has a brain tumor, it will be located in a certain area of the picture. You know approximately how much time he has left and also if he is going downhill or uphill and you know his unfinished business.

We have done this with thousands of children. We have even done it with children who later were murdered and with children who later were killed by sharks or by other accidents. Much of their awareness of their impending death is subconscious, coming from the spiritual quadrant.

The reason why children always know better than grownups is that they have not yet been contaminated by negativity. If you raised the next generation with unconditional love and no punishment *ever*, but firm, consistent discipline, your next generation would need practically no healers because they would be able to heal themselves. They would be whole the way God created all of us.

You are always whole if you are in harmony between the physical, the intellectual, the emotional and the spiritual quadrants. You will experience traumas, naturally, and genetic defects will still be there.

If you raised children only with the natural emotions, and allowed them to externalize their pain, their anger, their grief, they would love to go to school. Learning would be a stimulating, challenging, exciting adventure, and the lessons would become very spiritual, because all this is within you. You are born from God, and your spiritual quadrant you don't have to shop for, pray for. It's given to you, it's a free gift. The only thing that blocks you from using it is your own negativity.

If it is indeed true that all children have all knowledge within —from your God inside of you, from your spiritual quadrant — then why do not grownups have it? How can we use this knowledge of children to help grownups?

I will now give you my favorite example to show in what sense the teaching of the symbolic language can be used to help grownups. I am using the example of cancer though I emphasize that in working with dying patients you should not emphasize cancer patients alone. People who have neurological diseases, multiple sclerosis, amyotrophic lateral sclerosis, people who have had strokes and can't speak or move anymore need just as much if not *more* help. We always talk of cancer patients as if cancer was the greatest tragedy in the world. I hope that you understand that I mean that we should help not only cancer patients but *all* people.

Bernie Siegel

We had a physician who came to our workshop who was very impressed with our use of spontaneous drawings with dying children. About two years ago he had the courage to be labeled a fool, to be called — he is called now a heretic... he is called... well, he got another nice label. We challenged him by sharing with him that we truly believe that this gift of inner knowledge is true not only with terminally ill children but also with entirely healthy grownups. After the diagnosis of a potentially terminal illness is verified, you simply ask the patient to draw a picture — no instructions, nothing else — just to give you an impression of where this person is at this time. Then after you have this impression you ask them to conceive of their cancer.

This physician took those drawings, went home and said, "OK, I will try to do what you say works."

Instead of telling his cancer patients what they ought to do, he gives them unconditional love and respect. And he puts no expectations on them and no claims. He says to his patients, "Draw me a picture!" The patients draw a picture, and then he knows where they are at, not only from the physical quadrant, but also from the emotional, spiritual, intellectual quadrants.

My dream picture — I have to brag about that — was a man who was diagnosed as having cancer *(shows a drawing to audience)*, and I will describe it for those of you who can't see it. After the patient had drawn a general picture — from which you can make a general evaluation of him — he was asked to conceive of his cancer. He drew a man — I am only drawing a symbolic body here — and in his body he drew big red concentric circles, meaning a body full of big red (danger color) cancer cells.

When he was asked to conceive of chemotherapy, which in this case was the treatment of choice that the oncologist had elected, and which I think most physicians would have recommended in this case, he drew big black arrows, each arrow hitting a cancer cell.

But there was a very odd and unexpected thing about his drawing. As the chemotherapy black arrows hit those red cancer cells each arrow deflected away from it.

Chemotherapy

If you didn't know anything about the interpretation of drawings and you were this patient's physician, would you have put him on chemotherapy? Would you have regarded him as a good candidate for this kind of treatment?

This patient was considered to be a good candidate for chemotherapy. Nevertheless, something inside this man — but not his intellect — told me that internally he knew that he was going to reject the chemotherapy that was offered him.

Now, the patient's message comes from a quadrant that is not yet considered reality by most of humanity. Because from our own intellectual, hypertrophic quadrant that considers itself to know everything better than the patient does, we consider this man to be silly, because it is statistically verified that this cancer responds beautifully to this type of chemotherapy. Therefore, the patient should be given it.

But when you look at what the patient's intuitive quadrant is saying, you can see that in this case chemotherapy just won't work.

So unconditional love — love which is not schmaltzy and sentimental — means: I respect my neighbor as myself. I respect people who have a knowledge about themselves that is beyond *my* knowledge of them. *Their* knowledge comes from a different quadrant but nevertheless it is always more accurate than what comes from the intellectual quadrant.

If I can respect that and know that, I can ask this man, "What did your doctor tell you about this chemotherapy?" This man answers, "My doctor told me that the chemotherapy kills my cancer cells." And I say, "*Yes!*" meaning, "Go on, get it!" And his face drops.

I think that I am missing something, so again I say, "What did your doctor tell you about the chemotherapy?" Again he says very matter of factly, "My doctor told me that the chemotherapy kills my cancer cells."

And this time I say, "Yes, *but*...?"

He looks at me as if he wants to check me out, and he says, "Thou shalt not kill."

And I say, "Huh?"

He repeats again, "Thou shalt not kill."

And now — understanding better — I say, "Not even your own cancer cells?" and he says, "No. You see Doctor Ross, I was raised as a Quaker. I truly believe in universal law: Thou shalt not kill. And I was thinking about it very seriously: No, I do not think that I can kill."

If you practice unconditional love, you respect your fellow man without trying to convince, convert or change him. So I had no problem telling him that I wished all people would believe in universal law, because then the world would be a very peaceful and beautiful place. This was an implicit expression of my respect for him and made it clear to him that I was not going to belittle him, laugh at him or criticize him. But then I had to add, "Do me a favor." You understand, I want all my patients to get well. I am not saying that to him, but that is what I am now trying to talk him into. I say, "Do me a favor. Go home, and conceive how you can get rid of your cancer." Do you understand the difference in wording? And he says, "That is a good idea."

And he leaves and a week later he comes back.

I ask him, "Were you able to conceive a way to get rid of your cancer, which really means how *we* can help you?" And he has again that gorgeous smile on his face. And he says, "Yep!" I said, "Draw me a picture!"

And his whole picture — and I am only drawing a single big one so you can see what it looked like — instead of being full of red cancer cells, the whole body of the man that he drew was now full of gnomes. These little guys, you know... (*draws a gnome at the blackboard. Amuse-*

ment from audience) ... every gnome was lovingly carrying away a cancer cell *(applause and happy laughter)*.

The Gnomes

I was very touched by him. I called his oncologist and told him this, and on the very same day, he put the patient on chemotherapy. Today this man is still well.

Do you see the beauty of this? It is to me an incredible opening of things. It only takes humility, the only thing it takes is to know that all of us have all the knowledge we need within, and if we are humble and open and respect and love our neighbors as ourselves, we can help each other.

And it doesn't take time. It takes five minutes and doesn't cost a nickel. I am not exaggerating.

I hope you understand that this is what we consider holistic medicine. I may have the intellectual knowledge of the malignancy. The patient *has his intuitive knowledge. And if we begin to work together and respect and help each other, then we can truly help each other to become whole.*

This is to me what healing is in our time. In some way it has to do with consciousness and I don't know how to put that. It has to do with openness. And you cannot be open and you cannot reach this knowledge and this understanding and this compassion and this unconditional love as long as you have a Hitler within you. So, doctor: *Heal thyself!* And you are all doctors. All of you have to have the humility to acknowledge all the negativity that you have inside of yourself, every day.

And if you could do that, if you could acknowledge what I learned in Maidanek...It was in Maidanek that the woman stepped out who had lost her entire family. It was she who said to me, "Don't you believe, Elisabeth, that in all of us there is a Hitler?"

Yes. And in all of us is also a Mother Theresa. You cannot become a Mother Theresa, symbolically speaking, if you do not have the courage to look at your Hitler and get rid of him.

So this is what I say to you: if you want to *heal* the world, then heal yourself, get rid of your Hitler within. Then you will become a whole human being the way God created you. Then you will have cosmic consciousness, you will have out of body experiences, you will have anything you need — but not what you want, thank God *(amusement from audience)*.

The Workshops

Some people asked about the workshops. The workshops are offered by Shanti Nilaya. We give workshops all over the world from California to Australia. We invite seventy-five people to spend one week with us, from Monday noon till Friday noon. About one third of them are terminally ill patients or parents of dying children, one third are physicians, clergy, social workers, counselors, nurses, and one third are regular people. And what we do with this group is to show all the participants how in five days they can look at their own unfinished business and get rid of it. And you understand, the younger you are when you do it the more fully you can live afterwards.

It's a very intense five day workshop, where usually the terminally ill patients begin to share their anguish and pain and their unfinished business, their grief, and they touch upon their own pool of repressed tears and anger and unfinished business. And then we help them to ventilate it and externalize it. And on the last night, Thursday night, we have a very moving ritual, where people are in front of an outdoor fireplace, usually with their own wine and bread, and they share with the group what they are willing to leave behind. And they do that symbolically with a pine cone, placing the negativity into it and throwing it into the fire.

When we have the courage to look at our own negativity and leave it behind, then we can become more like Mother

Theresa. You cannot sit on your negativity and think that you can meditate it away. That really does not work.

You will find more pain and anguish in a group of seventy-five people than you can ever imagine, once you don't see the front but what is deep down inside that pool of repressed anguish and agony. And the greatest grief you can ever experience, which is far greater than any loss that anybody ever talks about, is *the grief over love that you have never experienced.* That is the greatest grief. Most people in our society have never experienced unconditional love, except perhaps from a Grandma or a Grandpa.

The last five-day workshop, from which I am just coming, had seventeen suicidal patients, who came to the workshop as their last straw, with a threat that if it didn't help they would commit suicide. I told them not to do it before Friday afternoon *(laughter from audience).* That too is something that you have to take seriously, but you also have to make these people aware that we human beings are totally and solely and exclusively responsible for our own lives. So don't go around and cry on other people's shoulders and waste your energy on self-pity. It is you and your choices that bring you where you are at.

And we human beings should bless ourselves every single day because we are the only living creatures in this galaxy who have been given free choice. And after death, when most of you for the first time realize what life *here* is all about, you will begin to see that your life here is almost nothing but the sum total of every choice you have made during every moment of your life. Your thoughts, which you are responsible for, are as real as your deeds. You will begin to realize that every word and every deed affect your life and also touch thousands of other lives.

Christ

Just watch yourself when you get up in the morning and are grouchy. You make your husband or your wife miserable and they go to work and let it out on the secretary. Then the secretary lets it out on her husband. Your children go to school miserable. They kick the dog on their way out, beat up the other kids and end up in the principal's office. You should count once how one grouch getting up in the morning can make life miserable for so many people.

It is such little things that you can experiment with yourself. The next day — even if you feel grouchy — sing, yodel or whistle just long enough until they are out of the house *(laughter)*. And then you may beat a rubber hose on a mattress and let out your anger on an inanimate object.

And then at the end of the day, ask your spouse, your mate, your children what kind of a day they have had, and then you will begin to see that *you* can change your life with simple things. You do not need to go to India, and you do not need LSD or mescaline or psilocybin in order to change your life. And you do not need to do anything except to be responsible for your choices.

And do what Christ did after what the Bible calls "fighting Satan," which was nothing but fighting the Hitler within himself after the forty days of fasting. He was totally aware that he could be the ruler of Jerusalem, that he could change this very decadent place at that time. But he also knew that it would not last long. The highest choice that he had available was to be willing never to use his powers and to be willing even to give his life if he could help one fellow man to understand that death does not exist, that death is only a transition to a different form of living.

He did that very thing. He knew that people believed in him only as long as he performed miracles. The moment he disappeared they would start wondering again. He knew the difference between knowing and believing.

And so after his death he materialized for his friends and his disciples for three days and three nights. He ate with them, he talked to them, he shared with them. And then they knew.

And it was the knowing, not the believing, that gave them the courage to do what they needed to do.

Those of you who are willing to go through the forty days of fasting, symbolically speaking — that means going through hell, being labeled, ridiculed, knocked, criticized — and in spite of that take the highest choice, you will not regret it.

And again, to give you a *very* practical example:

Dougy again

A couple of years ago I went to visit a nine-year-old boy in Virginia who was dying of cancer. And before I left I told him that he must have many questions. I said, "I cannot make house calls in Virginia very often but if you have any questions, just write to me."

One day I got a letter from Dougy. The letter was a two liner, "Dear Dr. Ross, I have only one more question left. What is life and what is death and why do little children have to die? Love, Dougy."

Do you understand why I am prejudiced in favor of children? They cut through all the baloney (*laughter from audience*). So I wrote him a letter. And I couldn't write him, you know, big stuff. I had to write to him the way he wrote to me.

So I wrote like that. I used those gorgeous felt pencils that have twenty-eight colors, rainbow colors. And it didn't look right yet so I started to illustrate it. Then when it was finished I liked it so much I wanted to keep it. My rationalization was naturally, "Yes, you are entitled to keep it. You know, you really worked on this letter, and it soon will be five o'clock, and the post office will be closed, and your children will come home from school, and you'd better put dinner up," and all the excuses why it was OK to do that — to keep the letter. The longer the list of excuses, the more I knew that it was *not* OK. So I said, "Here I go round teaching always to take the highest choice. What is my highest choice now? My highest choice is to go right down to the post office and to let go of it, because I did it for him, not for me." So I walked to the post office and mailed it.

Dougy was very proud and very happy. He shared it with many other dying children. That, in itself would have been very beautiful.

But about five months later, in March, when his birthday came up, this rather poor family made a long distance phone call to me. Dougy got on the phone and said, "Dr. Ross, today is my birthday. You are the only one who had enough faith that I would have another birthday. And I need to give you a gift for my birthday. I couldn't think of what to give you. We have nothing. The only thing that comes to me"... ("the only thing that comes to me," that is the spiritual quadrant)... "the only thing that comes to me over and over is to give you your beautiful letter back *(happy laughter from audience)*. But on one condition!" (it wasn't unconditional love!) *(laughter from audience)* "On one condition: that you print it *(laughter from audience)* and make it available to other dying children."

A lot of things started to rush through my head: it is expensive, twenty-eight colors on each page *(laughter from audience)*, intellectual quadrant, thrifty Swiss, how can people afford it. All that was interfering so I said, "No!" to it. Instead I took the highest choice. And it is literally true: if you share of yourself without expectations you get back ten thousand times.

This was four and a half years ago. When Dougy died, the *Dougy Letter* had reached ten thousand dying children *(applause)*.

Differentiate between your intellect and your intuition. When you think, it is your intellect *(laughter)*. When you do what *feels* right, it is your intuition. Intuition comes fast, makes no sense, is totally illogical and feels terrific *(happy laughter and applause)*. If you follow your intuition you are always in trouble. But I have a favorite thing at Shanti Nilaya which I believe in more than I believe in anything else and that is: *"Should you shield the canyons from the windstorms you will never see the beauty of their carvings."*

And when you follow your intuition you become a canyon eventually — if you last. But it is wonderful. *(In a happy, peaceful voice):* I would not like to live in any other time, because it was never more difficult and never more rewarding.